D1644070

Send Me A Message

A step by step approach to business
and professional writing

Send Me a Message, 1st edition

Various guidelines and language charts are reprinted in this publication, courtesy of the University of Washington's English Language Programs (UW ELP). UW ELP provides both Internet-based and traditional classroom language courses to meet the needs of international students and other non-native English speak more information, see the UW ELP Internet website at http://www.depts.washington.edu/uwelp/.

5 6 7 8 9 10 QPD 08 07
ISBN 13: 978-0-07-295351-0
ISBN 10: 0-07-295351-9

4 5 6 7 8 9 10 QPD 08 07
ISBN-13: 978-0-07-111081-5 (ISE)
ISBN-10: 0-07-111081-X (ISE)

Editorial director: Tina B. Carver
Senior sponsoring editor: Thomas Healy
Production manager: Juanita Thompson
Developmental editor: Susan Johnson
Cover: GTS Companies
Interior design: GTS Companies

The McGraw-Hill Companies

Table of Contents

To The Teacher

With the expansion of global business and the Internet, communicating clearly in written English has become essential. No longer is writing in English relegated to one or two English experts within a company; individuals in a variety of positions need to be able to send e-mail, write a letter of inquiry, and communicate effectively in written English.

The step-by-step approach in *Send Me a Message* allows students to develop a core set of expressions and functional language forms that they can use to communicate clearly and appropriately in a variety of formats. Students learn about the mechanics of various forms of correspondence (format, salutations and closings, headings, etc.) as well as more "macro" topics, such as which style of writing to choose (their own or that of the reader), the impact of language choice on tone, and strategies for successful communication.

Although the writing tasks in the book are typical in business settings, the skills and functional language taught can be used in many common personal situations, such as asking about products online, discussing things in a chat room or online discussion, and thanking someone for a visit. Each unit and chapter can be used independently, but if the first unit is used before the rest, students will need less correction in their writing, since many writing tasks use the basic functions and conventions taught in the first unit.

Send Me a Message is appropriate for intermediate- to advanced-level students. At this level, students have already mastered sentence-level grammar. Few, if any, of the functions listed below are new to them, but models and task-based practice help students learn to use them appropriately in written communication. In addition, students appreciate learning the mechanics and guidelines for interacting effectively in writing.

Topics	Functions	Mechanics
• format of letters and e-mail	• explaining purpose	• greetings
• routine requests and inquiries	• requesting	• closings
• non-routine requests	• inquiring	• format of letters and e-mail
• complaints	• suggesting	• punctuation
• responses to requests, inquiries, and complaints	• complaining	• capitalization
• tone and language choice	• apologizing	• addresses and dates
• job-search writing: resumes, cover and follow-up letters	• responding to requests (positively and negatively)	• subject headings
	• expressing opinions	• reference lines
	• agreeing and disagreeing	
	• hedging	

Each lesson begins with models and a recognition task. Charts with guidelines and examples are followed by exercises to help students apply the guidelines. Each lesson ends with a free-writing task.

Acknowledgments

This book was developed from an online course in business writing that I wrote for the University of Washington. I'd like to thank Anita Sökmen and Bill Harshbarger for their support and encouragement while I wrote the original course and started working with McGraw-Hill on this text. I'd also like to thank all my colleagues who volunteered to review the drafts for the online course: Laurie Blackburn, Lisa Carscadden, Mark Christianson, Mihaila Giurca, Lanita Grice, Rich Hawkins, Karen Hayes, Patty Heiser, Ellie Holstein, Andrea Koehler, Kay Landolt, Jean Martone, William Morrill, Marshall Palmer, Michelle Sadlier, Donna Schaeffer, Fred Servito, Anita Sökmen, Mary Nell Sorensen, Gwen Stamm, Alison Stevens, and Donna Warren. Their comments were especially helpful in revising the guidelines in each lesson. Teachers who have used various versions of the materials in their classes have also encouraged me along the way: Candace Jarrett, Jennifer Altman, Wendy Asplin, Richard Moore, and Stephanie Sidhom. I'd also like to thank Barbara Hansen, who shared many creative ideas with me when we taught business English and wrote materials together in the 1980s.

At McGraw-Hill, I'd like to thank Erik Gundersen for putting me in touch with Thomas Healy, ELT Editor. It has been a pleasure to work with Thomas on this project.

As always, I'd like to acknowledge my husband, George, who is a great sounding board, and my daughter, Caroline, who with cheerful good nature takes my constant computer work in stride.

Evaluation Exercises

How much do you know about written communication in English? Complete these exercises. At the end of the course, you will do them again to see how much you have learned.

Letter

You are beginning an international training program. The program starts on September 15. Your sister just told you that she is getting married. The wedding is on September 16.

Write a letter to Joe Hogan (Hogan is his last name). He is the director of the International Training Program. Ask him if you can start the program one week late, on September 22. The address for the program is Box 354232, Seattle, WA 98195. Don't forget to include your return address and the date.

Evaluation Exercises

Exercise

2

Envelope

Write the addresses on the envelope for your letter. Don't forget to include your return address.

Exercise

3

E-Mail

You have questions about the program. You want to talk with your instructor, Anna Harrison. Write an e-mail message to your instructor to ask to meet. Suggest a time.

To: Anna Harrison <aharrison@ITP.org>
Subject: Meeting

Introduction: Basic Decisions

Exercise 1

Here are four examples of written communication. Try to describe them. As you read each one, check off the form, the tone, and the reader.

This is a(n)
____ letter
_√_ e-mail
____ note

The tone is
____ formal
____ informal

The reader is
____ a friend
____ a business
     acquaintance
____ a co-worker
____ a stranger

	A
From: Julie Methow <JulieMethow@home.com> Date: Tuesday, October 30, 200X 2:23 PM To: Dave Thompson <tracer38@earthlink.net> Subject: Local Distributor	
I've seen your website and would like to look at your products before ordering online. Do you have any distributors located in the Toronto area? Thank you, Julie Methow	
JulieMethow@home.com 806-848-3837	

This is a(n)
_____ letter
_____ e-mail
_____ note

The tone is
_____ formal
_____ informal

The reader is
_____ a friend
_____ a business
     acquaintance
_____ a co-worker
_____ a stranger

B

Morning Shift,

Could someone take the stack of B5-C packets to the mail room this morning? We couldn't get in there tonight —someone had already locked it when we finished the batch.

Thanks!

Fredericka

This is a(n)
____ letter
____ e-mail
____ note

The tone is
____ formal
____ informal

The reader is
____ a friend
____ a business
acquaintance
____ a co-worker
____ a stranger

ATCO   C
3500 Walnut Street
Philadelphia, PA 19130

April 4, 200X

Ms. Katerina Hogue
President, GRZ Productions
5351 5th Avenue
New York, NY 10001

Dear Ms. Hogue:

Thank you for your letter inquiring about our professional quality audio cassettes. I have enclosed the information that you requested.

We have a special introductory offer that you may be interested in. For a limited time, we are offering a 20% discount on orders of 500 or more blank cassettes.

Please let me know if you would like any more information about our products.

Sincerely yours,

Mark Sataloff

Mark Sataloff

Sales Associate, ATCO

ENC: brochure

This is a(n)
____ letter
____ e-mail
note

The tone is
____ formal
____ informal

The reader is
____ a friend
____ a business
acquaintance
____ a co-worker
____ a stranger

		D
From:	Julie Methow <JulieMethow@home.com>	
Date:	Tuesday, October 30, 200X 2:23 PM	
To:	Anna Ayestas <A_Ayestas@aol.com>	
Subject:	Lunch?	

Hi Anna,

Do you want to get together for lunch tomorrow? I'm free from 11:30. Bring your pictures, OK?

Julie

JulieMethow@home.com
806-848-3837

Decisions in Written Communication

As the examples show, there are many different ways to communicate. Every time you communicate in writing, you make decisions. Here are some typical questions writers may ask.

> How can I get the response I want?
> Should I write *Dear Mr. Smith* or *Dear John*?
> Do I use a comma (,) or a colon (:)?
> Is it all right to be informal when I write this e-mail message?

The guidelines and exercises in this book will help you make these choices and be successful in communicating in writing.

Guidelines	Examples
> Each form of written communication looks different. This is called **format**. Each format has different rules for greetings, closings, and punctuation.	E-mail Letter
> With all formats, your choice of **tone** affects how successful you will be. Tone is the feeling of the letter. Is it professional, friendly, or angry? Tone is very important to your success, because the reader responds to your tone.	Send me information. Could you send me information? I would appreciate it if you could send me information. Thanks! Thank you for your help.
> The **level of formality** is related to tone. It depends on your relationship with the reader.	Let me know, OK? I would appreciate it if you could let me know what you think.
> Every form of communication is different, but the same **functional language** is used in many types of communication. Here are four that you will use frequently.	requests suggestions apologies complaints